AF587602

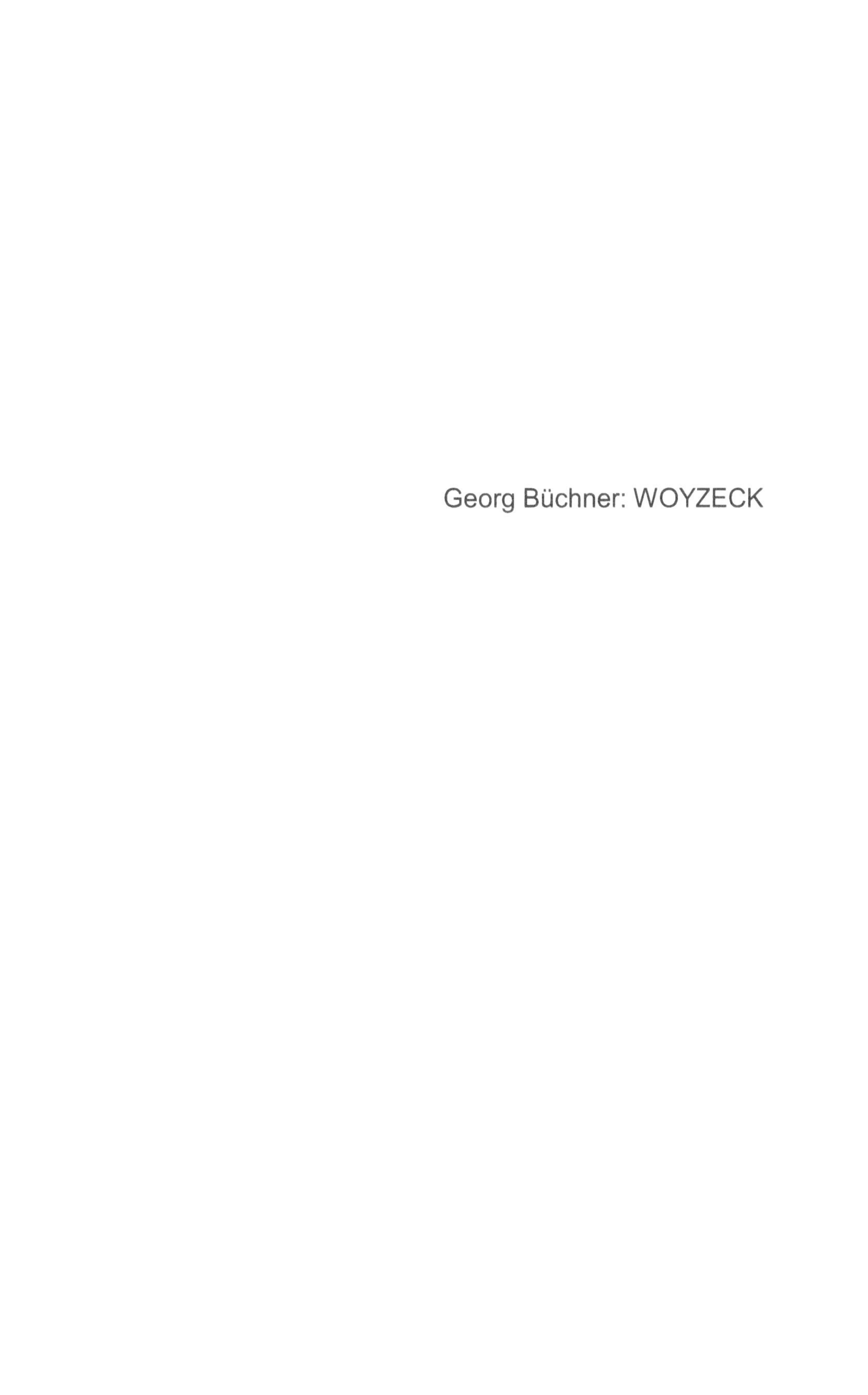

Georg Büchner: WOYZECK

Georg Büchner: WOYZECK

A new translation by Dan Farrelly

Carysfort Press

A Carysfort Press Book in association with Peter Lang

Georg Büchner: WOYZECK
In a new English translation by Dan Farrelly

First published in Ireland in 2004 as a paperback original by
Carysfort Press, 58 Woodfield, Scholarstown Road, Dublin 16
Ireland

ISBN 978-1-78997-113-2

Typeset by Carysfort Press
Cover design by Alan Bennis
Original photo for cover from the translator's collection
Printed and bound by eprint Ltd
35 Coolmine Industrial Estate, Dublin 15

The translation follows the edition of the *Studienausgabe* (Lese-und Bühnenfassung) edited by Burghard Dedner after the edition of Thomas Michael Mayer © 1999 Philipp Reclam jun. GmbH & Co., Stuttgart, Germany.

The publication of this work was supported by a grant from the Goethe-Institut.

Für Una

die Liebe, die Weise, die Ermutigende

Acknowledgements

I would like to thank the Arts Council and the Goethe-Institut Inter Nationes for their financial support towards the publication of this translation; Lilian Chambers and Eamonn Jordan of Carysfort Press for bearing with me during the long wait for the completion of the introduction; Ilse Nagelschmidt and Brigitte Jäger of Leipzig University for facilitating my visits to Leipzig and for helpful advice; Frau Doctor Linder of the Leipzig University Library for her generous help and advice; Frau Prell and Frau Ellender of the Goethe-Schiller Archive in Weimar for allowing me access to the original *Woyzeck* manuscripts as well as for alerting me to the very latest publications of German *Woyzeck* editions based on the original documents. Finally, my thanks are due to Lorraine Byrne for her careful reading of the manuscript. D.F.

Translator's Preface

Apart from fascination with the play itself, what has most induced me to undertake a translation of Büchner's *Woyzeck* is the conviction that, in the light of the newest scholarship, the play needs to be presented in a form which

1. highlights the **correct sequence of scenes**, and
2. explains the **scholarly basis** which confirms this sequence as the correct one.

The reader will not find here debate about the literary sources of Büchner's play, or discussion about where it fits into his oeuvre, or explanation about the intellectual world that Büchner inhabited. The book is consciously presented in such a way that, apart from the few short appendices, there is nothing to distract the reader from these two objectives.

INTRODUCTION

End of the fragment theory

Woyzeck - in productions, editions, translations - has always been the victim of the fragment theory. Had Büchner lived just one week longer, his *Woyzeck* would, almost certainly, never have been thought of - and treated as - a fragment. Though confident that he would within eight days[1] present a complete play to his publisher, as it happened, his death prevented this. Thus, what he bequeathed to the world was a group of four separate manuscripts of highly dramatic material based on the real-life story of Woyzeck.[2]

---

[1] Cf. Büchner's letter to Wilhelmine Jaeglé, Zurich, 1837: '[I'll] release *Leonce and Lena* along with two other dramas for publication in a week at most.' (...Ich werde in längstens acht Tagen *Leonce und Lena* mit noch zwei anderen Dramen erscheinen lassen) in *Georg Büchner, Complete Works and Letters*, ed. Walter Hinderer, trans. Henry J. Schmidt. (New York: Continuum, 1986), p.296.

[2] Büchner's original manuscripts ('Handschriften'), numbered H1, H2, H3, and H4, are kept in the Goethe-Schiller Archive in Weimar. There are also two excellent facsimile editions available. Cf.*Georg*

None of the four manuscripts contained a full sequence of scenes. Some scenes from the first manuscript were revised in the second, and some appeared, repeated or revised, in the fourth manuscript. The third manuscript contained two scenes which were not taken up into the later, fourth manuscript.

Faced with this seemingly disjointed collection of scenes, interpreters – for opera, stage and book – understandably have felt free to put their own shape on this highly dramatic material. It is equally understandable that drama theorists felt justified in aligning *Woyzeck* with what Brecht was later to refer to as 'non-Aristotelian theatre' – with its sequence of scenes which were linked into a story-line, or 'fable', but which did not build in a dramatic sequence of the kind we associate, broadly, with Aristotelian or classical theatre. *Woyzeck* came to be seen as an excellent example of open theatre and thereby as a forerunner of several trends in modern theatre.

The most recent (mainly German) scholarship, while highlighting the modernity of Büchner's treatment of his hero (or non-hero), his criticism of the oppressive social order, and hallucinatory and half-mystical elements in his writing, has at last been able to establish an authentic sequence of *Woyzeck* scenes as Büchner planned them

---

Büchner: Woyzeck. Faksimileausgabe der Handschriften, ed. Gerhard Schmid (Leipzig: Edition Leipzig, 1981); and *Georg Büchner: Woyzeck. Faksimile, Transkription, Emendation und Lesetext. Buch- und CD-ROM-Ausgabe*, ed. Enrico de Angelis (Munich: K.G. Saur, 2000).

shortly before his death.

Structurally, the play can no longer be simply regarded as a prime example of 'open' theatre. Of course, neither is it simply a continuation of the 'closed' classical tradition. While the dramatic structure is not at all complex, the dramatic line is extremely tight, and the drama moves inexorably, and with increasing momentum, to its inevitable climax in the death of Marie.

This new conception of the dramatic structure of *Woyzeck* is an invitation and a challenge to producers and directors of theatre to re-think their ideas about how the play is to be performed. With plays the text of which has been clearly established and which have been produced countless times with great respect for the author's intentions it makes sense to try something 'different' – as with the many and varied productions of Shakespeare's plays. But with *Woyzeck*, which the productions have – because the text has traditionally been seen as a conglomeration of dramatic fragments – never presented the way its author intended, it is time to see what this newly established understanding of the play demands of director and actors. If Beckett, for example, had the right to insist that his conception of the play be always respected, one can argue that Büchner, too, now that his structural plan for the play has been firmly established, has the right to authentic productions.

Solving the jigsaw puzzle

Büchner died of typhoid fever in 1837. In 1850, his brothers Ludwig and Alexander laboured with difficulty at deciphering large sections of the *Woyzeck* manuscripts but decided for a variety of reasons not to publish them. In 1875, the Austrian writer Karl Emil Franzos made his attempt. He published part of the material in 1875. By 1880 he had published all of it in a *Collected Works* of Büchner, calling the play *Wozzek*. For all its failings, including the wrong spelling, this first edition was an important beginning and has exerted an influence on many future editions up to the present day. It was also the basis for Alban Berg's famous *Wozzeck* opera composed in 1925.

Georg Witkowski's 1920 edition corrected Franzos's arbitrary editorial decisions and mistaken text readings. Witkowski's improvements were also reflected in Fritz Bergemann's edition in 1922 – where the sequence was largely correct – but, curiously, in his 1926 revision of the edition Bergemann reverted to the previous, faulty scene sequence. Further scholarly editions – by Werner R. Lehmann in 1967, Egon Krause in 1969, Georg Schmid in 1981, Thomas Michael Mayer in 1990, and Henri Poschmann in 1992 – have re-established the correct sequence.

Discrepancy

It was at a performance of *Woyzeck* at the Residenztheater in Munich in 2000 that I bought the newest edition of the play – the 1999 Reclam edition of the *Studienausgabe*.[3] edited by Burghard Dedner following Thomas Michael Mayer's 1990 edition. Ironically, this Munich production, directed by Stéphane Braunschweig, had taken absolutely no account of the recent scholarship, entitling the play *Woyzeck*, with the subtitle: *Ein Fragment*. Braunschweig, since 2000 Director of the Théâtre National de Strasbourg, was content to base his production 'on the various sketches of the fragment' (auf mehreren Entwurfsstufen des Fragments). It was as if the finest and most meticulous work of the editors counted for nothing.

Not open theatre

It has been a commonplace in modern theatre theory to look on *Woyzeck* as an important anticipation of open theatre, culminating, above all, in the episodic theatre of Bertolt Brecht. The newest scholarship now makes this view untenable.

Erwin Scheuer, whose book on dramatic form in Büchner appeared in 1929 and has been quoted by most scholars dealing with the subject of closed and open

---

[3] *Georg Büchner: Woyzeck. Studienausgabe*. Nach der Edition von Thomas Michael Mayer herausgegeben von Burghard Dedner. (Stuttgart: Philipp Reclam jun., 1999). This edition is hereafter referred to as 'Dedner'.

theatre, had used Fritz Bergemann's 1922 Leipzig edition, which improved on earlier editions by following the correct sequence of scenes. Though Scheuer thus based his theorizings on a correct sequence, he still looked on Büchner as 'the one amongst the great German dramatists in whose work the open form is most developed'.[4] In discussing the German ballad tradition, Scheuer claims that the ballad tends to create [isolated] scenes.[5] This tendency towards forming a succession of [discrete] scenes is, he claims, fully realized in *Woyzeck*.[6] Benno von Wiese, whose volume *Die deutsche Tragödie von Lessing bis Hebbel* has been used by generations of students and scholars since it first appeared in 1948, is clearly influenced by Scheuer's views,[7] and refers to the '*Woyzeck* sketches with their technique of a loosely linked series of images [scenes]'.[8] Since he uses the Insel-Verlag edition, Leipzig, 1940, von Wiese's theorizings did not have the benefit of the new scholarship.

---

[4] Cf. Erwin Scheuer, *Akt und Szene in der offenen Form des Dramas dargestellt an den Dramen Georg Büchners*. Germanische Studien 77 (Berlin, 1929), p.16: 'derjenige unter den großen deutschen Dramatikern, der die offene Form am höchsten ausgebildet hat.'

[5] ibid., p.62. 'Die Ballade tendiert also zur Bildung von Scenen.'

[6] ibid.

[7] Benno von Wiese, *Die deutsche Tragödie von Lessing bis Hebbel*, (Hamburg: Hoffmann und Campe,1948). 7th impr. 1967, p.529. 'Die Skizzen zum *Woyzeck* mit ihrer lose aneinanderreihenden Bildertechnik, in denen sich eine an die Volksballade erinnernde Begebenheit in immer wieder wechselnden Bildern spiegelt...'

[8] Cf. Erwin Scheuer's reference to the balladesque, p.62.

In *Das epische Theater*, a very influential work on modern theatre, Marianne Kesting claimed that Büchner was one of the direct forerunners of modern epic theatre.[9] Referring to the structure of the play she says that the hunted character of the poor creature Woyzeck is portrayed by a rapidly changing series of fleeting scenes in the Expressionist manner, the capturing of images portraying concrete circumstances; the illumination of situations; and the creation of dark, threatening moods.[10] Volker Klotz, in his authoritative German work on closed and open drama, uses *Woyzeck* as an important example of modern 'open' theatre.[11] He based his theorizing on the out-of-date edition of F. Bergemann, 7th impression, Wiesbaden, 1958. The handicap of working with an inadequate edition (though possibly the best available at the time) can be seen where Klotz uses the structure of *Woyzeck* as an example that in open theatre the plot plunges 'in medias res', which means it begins with the scene where Woyzeck is shaving the Captain. This is what he gleaned from the Bergemann edition, whereas the

[9] Marianne Kesting, *Das epische Theater: zur Struktur des modernen Dramas, 3rd revised edition* (Stuttgart: Kohlhammer, 1967), p.27. '...[In] seiner Bedeutung rechnet er [Büchner] unter die unmittelbaren Vorbereiter des modernen epischen Theaters.'

[10] This is a paraphrase of Kesting's dense German text: '[Das] Gehetzte der armen Kreatur Woyzeck malt sich in einer schon an die expressionistische Bildertechnik gemahnende Szenenflucht, Niederschlägen von zuständlichen Bildern, Situations-beleuchtungen, düsteren, unheilgeladenen Stimmungen...', p.29f.

[11] Volker Klotz, *Geschlossene und offene Form im Drama*, 3rd edn. (Munich: Carl Hanser Verlag, 1968).

authentic sequence first shows the events of the night before: Woyzeck with Andres in the field; the visit of Woyzeck to Marie after the parade; and Woyzeck's visit with Marie to the circus. Woyzeck shaves the Captain first thing the next morning, which is the way his day usually begins.

Following Bergemann's edition with its displaced scenes, Klotz arrived at conclusions which the newer scholarship does not support: 'The world invades him from all sides and, instead of the linear thrust of the plot in closed theatre, creates a circular movement.'[12] As opposed to this, the text now established by the scholars shows the opposite with regard to *Woyzeck*.

Gabrielle Steinbach's very recent book for students of German at Abitur level[13] shows how difficult it has been for the implications of modern research to make an important impact, even on teachers. While the author is aware that Werner Lehmann's 1967 edition is the first historical-critical edition[14], she does not use it as a basis for her interpretation of *Woyzeck*. The text she uses appears at first sight to be modern enough – Reclam 2001 – but this is, in fact, identical with the 1952 Reclam

---

[12] 'Von allen Seiten dringt die Welt auf ihn ein, und schafft an Stelle des linearen zielstrebigen Handlungsverlaufs im geschlossenen Drama hier eine Kreisbewegung (besonders deutlich in 'Baal' und 'Napoleon', aber auch in 'Woyzeck'), ibid., p.115.

[13] Gabrielle Steinbach, Interpretationshilfe Deutsch. Georg Büchner, 'Woyzeck' (Freising: Stark, 2002).

[14] ibid., p.9.

edition (Universal-Bibliothek No. 7733). Thus she forms ill-founded conclusions: not surprisingly, she refers to Büchner's 'fragment technique' (Fetzentechnik)[15] with its loose arrangement of many individual scenes. For Steinbach, the drama unfolds spontaneously in separate scenes which have no cohesion amongst themselves. Unlike in traditional theatre, it is left to the spectator to find the connections and to identify the connecting thread of the plot.[16]

It is even more surprising that Michael Patterson, one of the very few English-speaking scholars[17] to have shown a clear appreciation of and to have contributed to the newest *Woyzeck* scholarship, in the year 2000 produced an edition in which the *Woyzeck* version does not at all follow the by then established views. In his collection *Büchner: The Complete Plays*, he writes: 'This present translation is the first in English to take account of the latest research on Büchner. (Although it was equally available to Victor Price, the translator of the Oxford

---

[15] ibid., p.36.

[16] ibid. 'Das Geschehen entfaltet sich spontan in jeder Szene für sich und unzusammenhängend; der Zuschauer wird anders als im traditionellen Theater gefordert, die die Handlung strukturierenden Verbindungen selbst zu erkennen und den roten Faden auszumachen.'

[17] Michael Patterson, ed., *Büchner: The Complete* Plays (London: Methuen Drama, 2000). Cf. also John Guthrie, *Georg Büchner: Woyzeck* (Bristol: Bristol Classical Press, 2nd edn 1993), who recognizes that there is a correct sequence of scenes. On this basis he has published an edition of the German text with English commentary, but there is no English translation based on it.

University Press volume *The Plays of Georg Büchner*, his translation is based on the obsolete Bergemann edition.)'[18] Then, of his own edition he writes: 'That is not to say that our own translator, John Mackendrick, has confined himself rigorously to the text as proposed in the above ordering of scenes. He has in fact taken up material from H1, H2, and H3 [the earlier manuscripts] which Büchner probably did not intend to use.'

Unfortunately, because of the interpolations from earlier manuscripts, the English translation in Patterson's edition has brought us no further, despite his own intimate knowledge of the newest scholarship.

But Patterson clearly makes the point that most concerns us here: 'Thanks to the researches of Lehmann (1967) and Krause (1969) we are at last in possession of as philologically accurate a text of *Woyzeck* as we can now hope for. [...] Since this last draft [H4], unlike the earlier three, was in a reasonably legible hand and since it is almost certain from Büchner's last letter to his fiancée[19] that he intended to complete *Woyzeck* within eight days, it is fair to assume that this H4 manuscript is, up to the point where it breaks off, an authentic record of Büchner's intentions with regard to the final version of the text.'[20]

---

[18] Patterson, p.172.

[19] See above, footnote 1.

[20] Patterson, p.167.

Conclusion

The scholars have established that H4 accounts for the first 17 scenes of the play and that the remainder (Scenes 18-25) is supplied by H1. A glance at the time-frame of these scenes[21] shows that all twenty-five of them take place in quick succession:

1-3	on the first evening
4-8	the following morning
9-12	probably in the afternoon of the same day
13	that night
14-17	the following day.
18-24	afternoon and evening of the same day.

It is interesting that the nature of this sequence reveals not only a tight unity of plot but also a tight (48-hour) unity of time, which aligns it with *closed* rather than with *open* theatre.

Following Dedner's 1999 edition, the present translation omits the entertaining scene featuring the Professor's lecture [H3,1]. Lehmann puts it after scene 17, where Woyzeck gives away his things to Andres (a last will and testament), and before the scene where Woyzeck takes Marie off to murder her. But, as Dedner argues,[22] why would he attend the Professor's lecture at this juncture? Poschmann places this scene after Scene 3 and

[21] Dedner, p.202ff.
[22] Dedner, p.205.

before the following (early) morning meeting with Marie, after which he races off to shave the Captain and later visit the doctor. It is not included in the seventeen scenes of H4. It seems that Scene 8, with the Doctor, has made the 'Professor's lecture' redundant. Similarly, following Dedner, the present translation omits the 'final' scene involving the Idiot, the Child and Woyzeck.[23]

The advance made by Dedner's edition can be illustrated by comparison with the fine, earlier work of Walter Hinderer in his 1986 edition with a translation by Henry J. Schmidt.[24] Hinderer follows the by now accepted convention of completing the H4 sequence by recourse to the later scenes of H1. He refers to 'Woyzeck. A Reconstruction. Consisting of Büchner's incomplete revision (Fourth Draft), scenes from the First Draft, and two optional scenes.' At this point Hinderer still envisages the inclusion – somewhere – of the popular H3,1, without sharing Dedner's later conviction that this scene has no valid place in the scene sequence.[25]

Note: Hinderer's 'Reconstruction' seems to be primarily an admirable scholarly enterprise rather than an attempt to present a text for stage production. Hence, where a sizeable gap occurs in the H4 manuscript in Scene 9,

---

[23] Dedner does, however, envisage the possibility of using this as an alternative ending. Cf. p.186.

[24] Hinderer, p.199.

[25] Dedner, p.205.

Hinderer does not fill it, whereas Dedner fills it by drawing on H2,7. Another gap in the H4 manuscript is that left after the mere title of Scene 3. This scene is indispensable. Both Hinderer and Dedner fill it in their own way by recourse to different parts of H1 and H2. A further indication that Hinderer is less concerned than Dedner with the staging of the play is that in his introduction he does not deal with the important issue of 'open' and 'closed' theatre.

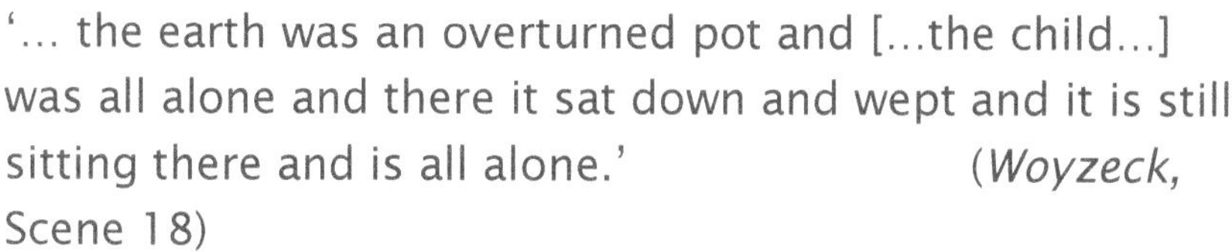

'... the earth was an overturned pot and [...the child...] was all alone and there it sat down and wept and it is still sitting there and is all alone.' (*Woyzeck*, Scene 18)

Characters

Franz Woyzeck
Marie Zickwolf
Christian, her child, about one year old
Captain
Doctor
Drum Major
Sergeant
Andres
Margaret
Announcer outside a booth
Old Man
Dancing Child
First Journeyman
Second Journeyman
The Idiot Karl
The Jew
Grandmother
First Child
Second Child
First Person
Second Person
Innkeeper
Cathy
Court Clerk
Barber
Doctor
Judge
Policeman

Soldiers, journeymen, people, girls, and children.

Scene 1 Open fields. The town in the distance.

***Woyzeck** and **Andres** are in the bushes cutting sticks.*

Woyzeck: Yeah, Andres, that strip over the grass, that's where the head rolls in the evenings. Someone picked it up once. Thought it was a hedgehog. Three days and three nights later he lay in his coffin. (*Softly*) Andres, it was the Freemasons! I've got it! The Freemasons! Sshh!

Andres: (*Sings*)

> Over there the two hares sat
> Chewing the green green grass

Woyzeck: Sshh! Something's there!

Andres:

> Chewing the green green grass
> Down to the ground

Woyzeck: It's moving behind me, under me. (*Stamps his foot on the ground*) It's hollow, do you hear? It's all hollow down there. The Freemasons.

Andres: I'm scared.

Woyzeck: So strangely quiet. You want to hold your breath. Andres!

Andres: What?

Woyzeck: Say something! (*Stares out in front of him*) Andres! It's bright! Fire's moving round the sky, a noise comes down like trumpets. It's looming up! Let's go! Don't look back. (*Drags him quickly into the bushes*)

Andres: (*After a pause*) Woyzeck! Hear it still?

Woyzeck: Quiet, everything's quiet, as if the world was dead.

Andres: Hear it? The drums. We have to go.

Scene 2

Marie** with her child at the window. **Margaret**. The parade goes by, led by the **Drum Major.

Marie: (*Dandling the child on her arm*) Laddy, jaa da da daah! Hear it? Here they come.

Margaret: What a man! Like the trunk of a tree.

Marie: He's standing there like a lion.

***Drum Major** greets her.*

Margaret: Well, what a glint in your eyes! That's new for you.

Marie: (*Sings*)

Soldiers, they are handsome fellows.

Margaret: The glint is still in your eyes!

Marie: So? Take yours to the Jew. Get them polished. Perhaps they'll sell as two buttons.

Margaret: What? Why, you…! I'm a respectable person, I am. But *you*! With your eyes you'd see through seven pairs of leather trousers.

Marie: Bitch! (*Slams the window shut*) Come, laddy. What do people want? You're just the poor little son of a whore. You make your mother happy with your dishonest-looking face. La! La!

Sings:

Lassie, what are you to do?
You have a child but not a husband
Ah, well, what's the worry?
I sing through the night,
Hi diddle dee my lad, diddle dee
What do they do for me? – Not a thing!

Johnnie harness your six horses now
Give them something to eat
They eat no oats
They drink no water
Nothing but cool wine for them, diddle dee
Nothing but cool wine for them.

A knock at the window.

Marie: Who's that? That you, Franz? Come in!

Woyzeck: Can't. There's a roll-call.

Marie: What's wrong, Franz?

Woyzeck: (*Mysteriously*) Marie, it happened again. A lot. Isn't it written, 'and behold, smoke went up from the earth like smoke from the oven'?

Marie: Franz!

Woyzeck: It followed me as far as the town. What'll come of it?

Marie: Franz!

Woyzeck: I have to go. (*He goes*)

Marie: Poor man. So haunted. He didn't look at his child. His thoughts will destroy him. Why so quiet, laddy? Afraid? It's becoming so dark, it's like being blind. Any other time the lantern shines in. I can't stand it. It sends shivers down my spine. (*Exit*)

Scene 3 Booths. Lights. People

***Old Man**. **A Child** dancing.*

> In the world there's nothing sound
> Everyone must die, we know it very well.

Woyzeck: Hop! Hop! Poor man, old man! Poor child, young child.[26] Hey, Marie, will I carry you? You have to push to the front if you want to eat. The world, a lovely world!

Announcer: (*Outside a booth*) Gentlemen, ladies, here you can see the astronomical horse and the common little

---

[26] Much of the text in this speech of Woyzeck is indecipherable.

fancy birds, favourites of all the potentates of Europe, and members of all learned societies. They can tell you everything: how old you are, how many children, your illnesses; can fire a pistol, stand on one leg. It's all education, they have only bestial reason, or rather, completely reasonable bestiality. Not individuals dumb as animals like plenty of people – leaving aside yourselves, of course! It's about to happen. The commencement of the commencement is about to begin. Gentlemen, gentlemen! Look at living creatures as God made them: nothing, nothing at all. Now look what art does: they walk on their hind legs, wear jacket and trousers and carry a sabre! Ha! Make a bow! Good boy. Give us a kiss! (*He makes a trumpeting gesture*) Mickey is musical. Look at the progress of civilization. Progress everywhere. A horse, a monkey, a canary. The monkey has turned into a soldier – not much of a thing, the lowest form of human life. Let the show begin. Let's start the beginning. Straight away the commencement of the commencement.

Woyzeck: Want to?

Marie: O.K. by me. Should be fun. Look at his tassles! And she's got trousers.

Sergeant. Drum Major.

Sergeant: Here, stop! Look at her! What a woman!

Drum Major: A devil made for producing regiments of cavalry and for breeding drum majors.

Sergeant: Look at her, head up – you'd think her black hair would drag it down like a weight. And her eyes – black.

Drum Major: Like looking down a well or a chimney. In there behind her.

Marie: Look at the lights.

Woyzeck: Yeah, a big black cat with fiery eyes. Hey, what an evening.

Inside the booth.

Barker: Show your talent. Show your bestial rationality. Make these humans blush. Gentlemen, this animal, as you see, with his tail and on all fours, is a member of all learned societies, professor at several universities where he teaches students to ride and fight. All that with simple reason. Think now with double reason. What do you do when you use your double reason? In this learned gathering is there an ass? (*The horse shakes his head*) Here you see the double reason at work.[27] This is not just an individual, a dumb animal. It's a person! A human being. A rational animal. But still an animal, a beast! (*The horse becomes unduly excited*) All right, so make them blush. You see, the beast is still nature, unspoiled nature. Learn from him. Ask the doctor. Dangerous teaching. They used to say man is natural, made of dust, sand and muck. You want to be more than dust, sand and muck? Take a look at reason. It can count, but it can't count on its

---

[27] Omitted here is: 'Das ist Viehsiognomik' (That's physiognomy). The deliberately corny pun in the German cannot be adequately reproduced in English.

fingers. Why? Just can't express itself, give explanations. It's a transformed human being. Tell the gentlemen what time it is! Which of the gentlemen and ladies has a watch? A watch?

Drum Major: A watch! (*Draws a watch ceremoniously from his pocket*) There you are.

Marie: I have to see this. (*Climbs onto the front seat.* ***Drum Major*** *helps her*)

Scene 4

Marie *sits with her child on her lap. She is holding a mirror fragment in her hand.*

Marie: (*Looking in the mirror*) The stones are brilliant! What sort are they? What did he say? – Sleep, laddie. Close your eyes, tight. (*The child covers his eyes with his hands*) Tighter. Stay like that, quiet, otherwise he'll come for you.

Sings: Lassie, close the shutters
A gypsy's on his way,
Leads you by the hand
Away to gypsy land.

(*Looks in the mirror again*) It's definitely gold! The likes of me has just a small corner in the world and a bit of mirror, and yet I have a mouth as red as the great ladies with their full-length mirrors and the fine gentlemen to kiss their hands. Just a poor woman. (*The child sits up*) Sshh, laddie, close your eyes, sleepy angel. Look at it run along the wall. (*Makes the glass reflect*) Close your eyes or it will look into you and you'll go blind.

***Woyzeck** enters behind her. Startled, she puts her hands to her ears.*

Woyzeck: What's wrong?

Marie: Nothing.

Woyzeck: Under your fingers – something shining.

Marie: A little earring. I found it.

Woyzeck: I've never found anything like that. Two at once.

Marie: Am I a whore?

Woyzeck: It's O.K., Marie. – The boys's fast asleep. Free his little arm from the chair. Beads of perspiration on his forehead. Life is only work. You even sweat in your sleep.That's the worst of being poor. Marie, there's some more money. My wages and a bit extra from the Captain.

Marie: God bless you, Franz.

Woyzeck: Have to go. See you this evening, Marie.

Bye.

Marie: (*Alone. After a pause*) I'm such a bad person. I could take a knife to myself. Ah, this life! Everything's going to the devil, man and woman.

Scene 5

*The **Captain**. **Woyzeck**. **Captain** seated. **Woyzeck** is shaving him.*

Captain: Take it easy, Woyzeck, take it easy. One thing at a time. You make me quite dizzy. What am I to do with the ten minutes if you finish early? Woyzeck, think about it. You've another thirty lovely years to live, thirty years! That's 360 months – and days, hours, minutes! What do you want to do with this monstrous amount of time? Organize yourself, Woyzeck.

Woyzeck: Yes, Captain, sir.

Captain: I get really worried about the world when I think of eternity. Being busy, Woyzeck, busy. Eternal, that's eternal, that's eternal; you can see that; then again it's not eternal – and *that*'s a moment, yes, a moment. Woyzeck, it makes me shudder when I think the earth revolves in a day. What a waste of time! Where's it leading to? Woyzeck, I can't even *look* at a mill-wheel any more or I become melancholy.

Woyzeck: Yes, Captain, sir.

Captain: Woyzeck, you always look so hunted. A good man doesn't do that, a good man with a good conscience. Talk to me, Woyzeck. What's the weather like today?

Woyzeck: Bad, Captain, sir, bad. Windy.

Captain: I can feel it. There's such quick movement out there. A wind like that has the same effect on me as a mouse. (*Jauntily*) I think it's coming from the south-north.

Woyzeck: Yes, Captain, sir.

Captain: Ha! ha! ha! South-north! Ha! Ha! Ha! So dumb, so disgustingly dumb. (*Moved*) Woyzeck, you are a good man, a good man – but (*with dignity*) you have no morality. Morality is when you are moral, understand? It's a good word. You have a child without the Church's blessing as our reverend garrison chaplain says: 'without the Church's blessing'. They're not my words.

Woyzeck: Captain, the dear Lord won't look to see if the poor little devil had the 'Amen' said over him before he was made. The Lord said, 'Let the little children come to me'.

Captain: What's that you said? What sort of strange answer is that? You're making me all confused with your answer.

Woyzeck: Poor people. You see, Captain, money, money. People with no money. People like me don't come into the world morally. We're made of flesh and blood. People like us have it bad in this world *and* the other. I reckon, if we go to heaven we'll have to help with making thunder.

Captain: Woyzeck, you have no virtue, you are not a virtuous person. Flesh and blood? When I lie by the window, when it has rained and I look at the white stockings as they leap across the streets – damn it all, Woyzeck – love comes over me. I've got flesh and blood, too. But, Woyzeck, virtue, virtue! How am I to pass the time? I always say to myself: you are a virtuous man, (*moved*) a good man, a good man.

Woyzeck: Yes, Captain, virtue. I haven't worked it out yet. You see, ordinary people, people like us have no virtue. Nature takes over. But if I was a gentleman, if I had a hat and a watch and a top coat and fine words, I'd like to be virtuous too. Virtue must be a great thing, Captain. But me, I'm just a poor devil.

Captain: Good, Woyzeck. You are a good man, a good man. But you think too much. It's draining you. You always look so hunted. This talk has got to me. Go off now, and don't be running! Slowly, nice and slowly down the street.

Scene 6 Street or lane

Marie. Drum Major.

Drum Major: Marie!

Marie: (*Looking at him expressively*) March up and down for me. A chest like a steer and beard like a lion. Never seen anything like it. I'm the proudest woman in the world.

Drum Major: On Sundays when I'm wearing the big plumed helmet and the white gloves, God! Marie, the Prince always says: 'Well, there's a man for you!'

Marie: (*Mocking*) Go on! (*Walks up to him*) What a man!

Drum Major: And what a woman you are. Jesus, let's start a brood of drum majors, eh? (*Puts his arms around her*)

Marie: (*Annoyed*) Let me go!

Drum Major: Wild animal.

Marie: (*Vigorously*) Dare touch me!

Drum Major: Is that the devil in your eyes?

Marie: Maybe. It's all the same.

Scene 7 Street or lane

Marie. Woyzeck.

Woyzeck: (*Stares at her, shakes his head*) Hm! I see nothing, nothing. You should be able to see it. Should be able to take hold of it with your hands.

Marie: (*Intimidated*) What's wrong, Franz? It's brain-fever, Franz.

Woyzeck: A sin so fat and wide. The stink is enough to smoke the angels out of their heaven. You have a red mouth, Marie. No blisters on it? Bye, Marie, you are as beautiful as sin. – Can mortal sin be so beautiful?

Marie: Franz, you're raving.

Woyzeck: The devil! – Did he stand there, like this, like this?

Marie: The whole day long and since the world began many people can stand in the one place, one after the other.

Woyzeck: I saw him.

Marie: You can see a lot if you have two eyes, are not blind, and the sun is shining.

Woyzeck: With his…

Marie: (*Cheekily*) Whatever.

Scene 8

Woyzeck**. The **Doctor.

Doctor: What's this, Woyzeck? A man of his word.

Woyzeck: What do you mean, Doctor?

Doctor: I saw it, Woyzeck. You pissed in the street, pissed on the wall like a dog. Yet you get tuppence daily. Woyzeck, that's bad. The world is going to the bad. It's very bad.

Woyzeck: But Doctor, when nature calls…

Doctor: Nature calls, nature calls! Nature. Haven't I demonstrated that the *musculus constrictor vesicae* is subject to the will? Nature! Woyzeck, man is free. In man, individuality is transfigured into freedom. Unable to hold his urine. (*Shakes his head, joins his hands behind his back and paces up and down*) Have you eaten your peas, Woyzeck? There's a revolution in science. I'm exploding it. Uric acid zero point ten, ammonium chloride, hyperoxide.[28] Woyzeck, don't you have to piss again? Go in there and try.

Woyzeck: I can't, Doctor.

Doctor: (*Pointedly*) But you can piss on the wall! I have it in writing. Here's the agreement in my hand. I saw it, saw it with my own eyes. I was just sticking my nose out the window and letting the sunrays enter to observe sneezing. (*Starts kicking him*) No, Woyzeck, I'm not annoyed.

[28] 'Hyperoduxul' – probably a meaningless term, which suggests that the doctor is a charlatan.

Annoyance is unhealthy. It's unscientific. I am calm, quite calm, my pulse has its usual sixty beats and I say it to you with the utmost objectivity. God forbid that I'd be annoyed about a human being. A human being! A proteus, maybe, if it dies on you. – But you shouldn't have pissed against the wall.

Woyzeck: Doctor, look, sometimes you have a sort of character, a sort of structure. But with nature it's different. You see, with nature (*He cracks his knuckles*) it's, how do you say it, for example…

Doctor: Philosophizing again, Woyzeck.

Woyzeck: (*Confidentially*) Doctor, have you seen anything of the double nature? In the midday sun, when it's as if the world is going to burst into flames, a terrifying voice has spoken to me.

Doctor: Woyzeck, you have an *aberratio*.

Woyzeck: (*Puts his finger to his nose*) The sponges, Doctor. There's the secret. Have you seen the shapes they grow in on the ground? If only we could read them.

Doctor: Woyzeck, you have the most beautiful *aberratio mentalis partialis*, second species – beautifully developed. Woyzeck, you get a supplement. Second species, idée fixe with generally rational condition. Doing everything as usual? Shaving the Captain?

Woyzeck: Yes.

Doctor: Eating your peas?

Woyzeck: Just as you've said, Doctor. I give the wife the money for it.

Doctor: Doing your job for the army?

Woyzeck: Yes.

Doctor: You're an interesting casus. Case Woyzeck gets a supplement. Keep it up. Show me your pulse! Yes.

Scene 9 Street or lane

Captain. Doctor.

Captain: Doctor, I feel afraid for horses when I think the poor beasts have to go everywhere on foot. Don't run like that. Don't wave your stick in the air like that. You trying to catch up with death? A good man with a good conscience doesn't walk so fast. A good man. (*He catches the doctor by the coat*) Doctor, allow me to save a human life. You're tearing along. Doctor, I am so melancholy, there's a rapturous side to me. I have to weep when I see my coat hanging on the wall. I see it hanging.

Doctor: Hm, bloated, fat, thick neck, apoplectic constitution. Yes, Captain, you could suffer an *apoplexia cerebralis*, but possibly just on the one side and then be paralysed only on one side. Your best chance is to be mentally paralysed and become a vegetable. Those are, more or less, your prospects for the next four weeks. Moreover, I can assure you that your case is one of the interesting ones, and if God wills it that your tongue becomes partially paralysed we can do the most glorious experiments.

Captain: Doctor, don't terrify me. People have died of fright, of sheer unadulterated terror. I can already see the people with their top hats in their hands – but they will say, he was a good man, a good man – the devil take you!!

Doctor: (*Holding out his hat*) What is that, Captain? – An empty head.

Captain: (*Making a crease in it*) What is that, Doctor? – A bent mind.

Doctor: Goodbye, pushups master.

Captain: Goodbye, coffin filler.

***Woyzeck** comes running along.*

Captain: Woyzeck, what are you rushing past me for? Stay a minute, Woyzeck. You run through the world like an open razor. We cut ourselves on you. You run as if a regiment of cossacks had to be shaved and you'd be hanged if every last hair hadn't been cut within the quarter hour. But, speaking of long beards, what was I going to say? Woyzeck, long beards…

Doctor: A long beard under the chin – it's mentioned as early as Pliny – soldiers should be discouraged from wearing them, who …

Captain: (*Continuing*) Speaking of long beards? How is it, Woyzeck? Not yet found a hair from one in your soup? You know what I mean, don't you, a human hair, from the beard of a soldier, a sergeant – a drum major? Eh, Woyzeck? But you've a good wife. Not like the rest.

Woyzeck: Yes. What are you saying, Captain?

Captain: What a face the fellow's making … But you don't have to look in your soup now. Hurry round the corner, perhaps you can find one on a pair of lips. A pair of lips,

Woyzeck. I have that love feeling again, Woyzeck. Hey, fellow, you're as pale as a ghost!

Woyzeck: Captain, I'm just a poor devil. I've got nothing else in the world, Captain. If you're joking …

Captain: Joking? Me joking – joking with you!

Doctor: Your pulse, Woyzeck, small, hard, hopping, uneven.

Woyzeck: Captain, the earth is hot as hell. To me it is ice-cold, ice-cold, hell is cold. I'll take a bet on it. Impossible. Man, man! Impossible.

Captain: Hey you! Do you want to be shot? Want a couple of bullets through your head? Your eyes – if looks could kill! – and I mean the best for you, because you are a good man, Woyzeck, a good man.

Doctor: Facial muscles stiff, tense, sometimes twitching, bearing upright and tense.

Woyzeck: I'm going. Anything is possible. People! Anything. Nice weather, Captain. When you look at such a solid grey sky you might want to drive a hook into it and hang yourself – just because of the hyphen between Yes and No, Yes and No. Yes and No, Captain? Is the No to blame for the Yes or the Yes for the No? I'll give it some thought.

***Woyzeck** goes off with long strides, first slowly then with increasing tempo.*

Doctor: (*Chasing after* him) A phenomenon, Woyzeck! Extra pay.

Captain: People make me quite dizzy. The long-legged fellow, what fast strides he makes – his shadow like a spindly spider – and the short one with his jerky little steps. The long one is the lightning and the short one the thunder. Ha, ha, one after the other. I don't like it! A good person is grateful and loves his life. A good person doesn't have courage. A villain has courage! I only went to war to bolster my love of life. From fear [...][29] to war, to courage! Grotesque where such ideas come from, grotesque!

Scene 10 The Guard room

Woyzeck. Andres.

Andres: (*Sings*)

My landlady has a good little maid
She sits in the garden night and day
She sits there in her garden.

Woyzeck: Andres!

Andres: What?

Woyzeck: Nice day.

Andres: Holiday weather and music in the open air. The women are out already, in a lather. It's on.

Woyzeck: (*On edge*) Dance. Andres, they're dancing.

Andres: In 'The Steed' and in 'The Star'.

Woyzeck: Dancing, dancing.

Andres: Sure, O.K.

---

[29] Indecipherable word in original text is omitted here.

She sits there in her garden
Until the clock strikes twelve
And watches out for soldiers.

Woyzeck: Andres, I'm all on edge.

Andres: You're mad.

Woyzeck: I have to go out. My head is spinning. What hot hands they have. Damn it, Andres!

Andres: What's wrong?

Woyzeck: Must go.

Andres: With that whore.

Woyzeck: Have to go, it's so hot in here.

Scene 11 Inn

Windows open, dancing. Benches in front of the inn. Lads.

First Journeyman:

The shirt I'm wearing
Isn't mine
My soul, it stinks, it reeks of wine.

Second Journeyman: Man, you want me, friendly like, to put a hole in you? God dammit! I want to put a hole in you. I'm quite a guy, you know. All the fleas on you, I'll kill 'em dead.

First Journeyman: My soul, it stinks, it reeks of wine. Even money rots away. Forget me not. What a lovely life it is. My tears could fill a rain barrel. I wish our noses were bottles. We could empty them down one another's throats.

The others: (*Singing in chorus*)

> There was a huntsman from the Pfalz
> Went riding through a forest green
> Halli, halloh, it's fun to hunt
> Around the blooming heather
> I'll do it any weather.

Woyzeck *takes up position at the window.* ***Marie*** *and the* ***Drum Major*** *dance past without noticing him.*

Marie: (*As she dances*) Keep it going, keep it going.

Woyzeck: (*Choking*) Keep it going, keep it going. (*Stands suddenly erect, sinks back onto the bench*) Keep it going, keep it going, (*Smacks his hands together*) turn in circles, roll around. Why doesn't God snuff out the sun to let everything in orgy, man and woman and animals as well, roll around on top of one another. They're doing it in broad daylight, they're doing it like insects on the back of your hand. Woman! The woman is hot, hot! Keep it going! Keep it going! (*Jumps up*) That fellow! His hands on her body, they're everywhere.

First Journeyman: (*Preaching on the table*) But when a traveller stands leaning on the stream of time or thinks of divine wisdom and addresses himself: Why does man exist? Why does man exist? But verily, I say to you: from what would the farmer, the cooper, the cobbler, the doctor live if God hadn't created man? From what would the tailor live if God hadn't implanted in man the feeling of modesty. From what would the soldier live if God hadn't equipped him with the need to get himself killed? Therefore, have no doubt. Yes, yes, it's pleasant and good, but everything on earth is vanity – even money rots away. And to conclude, my dear brethren, let us now piss on the cross so that a Jew will die.

Scene 12 Open field

Woyzeck: Keep it going, keep it going. Quiet, music. (*Stretches out on the ground*) What's that? What are you saying? Louder, louder, stab her, stab her to death? Am I to? Must I? Do I still hear it? Does the wind say it too? It's keeping up, stab her, stab her to death.

Scene 13 Night

***Andres** and **Woyzeck** in a bed.*

Woyzeck: (*Shakes **Andres***) Andres! Andres! I can't sleep. When I close my eyes my head spins and I hear the fiddles, keep it going, keep it going, it's coming out of the wall – don't you hear anything?

Andres: Yeah, let them dance. God preserve us. Amen. (*Falls asleep again*)

Woyzeck: It's cutting through my forehead like a knife.

Andres: You need some brandy and a pill, that'll kill the fever.

Scene 14 Inn

Drum Major*. *Woyzeck*. *People.

Drum Major: I'm a man! (*Beats on his chest*) A man, I tell you. Anything to say? If you're not drunk as a lord, keep away from me. I'll beat your nose up your arse-hole. I'll – (*To* ***Woyzeck***) here, you, drink, a man must drink, I wish the world was schnaps, schnaps. (***Woyzeck*** *whistles*) You want me to pull your tongue out and wrap it round your waist? (*They wrestle,* ***Woyzeck*** *loses*) Will I leave enough breath in you as an old woman's fart? Will I? (***Woyzeck*** *sits down on the bench. He is exhausted and shaking*) He can whistle till he's blue in the face.

Ha! Drinking brandy is my life
Brandy gives me courage.

One man: He was looking for it.

Another: He's bleeding.

Woyzeck: One thing follows the other.

Scene 15

*The **Jew.***

Woyzeck: The pistol's too dear.

Jew: It's up to you. Take it or leave it.

Woyzeck: The knife, how much?

Jew: It's in good shape. Want to cut your throat with it, that it? You can have it as cheap as anyone. Your death can be cheap but not for nothing. That it? An economical death.

Woyzeck: That'll cut more than bread.

Jew: Two pence.

Woyzeck: There! (*He leaves*)

Jew: There! As if it was nothing. But it is money. The dog!

Scene 16

***Marie**. The **Child**. The **Idiot**.*

Marie: (*Turning the pages of the Bible*) And no deceit is found in his mouth. God, God. Don't look at me. (*Turns more pages*) But the Pharisees brought to him a woman taken in adultery and they placed her in the midst. And Jesus said: Nor do I condemn thee. Go now and sin no more. (*Claps her hands together*) God, God. I can't. God, just give me strength to pray. (*The child nestles in to her*)

The child pierces my heart like a knife. (*To the* ***Idiot***) Get! Lazing around the place.

Idiot: (*Lying there reciting fairy stories using his fingers*) The king, he has the golden crown. Tomorrow I'll bring the queen her child. Blood sausage says: Come, liver sausage. (*He takes the child and falls silent*)

Marie: Franz didn't come home, not yesterday, not today. It's getting hot here. (*She opens the window*) She came in and cast herself down at his feet and wept and began to wash his feet with her tears and to dry them with the hair of her head. And she kissed his feet and anointed them with ointment. (*Beats her breast*) All dead! Saviour, Saviour, I would like to anoint your feet.

Scene 17 Barracks

Andres. ***Woyzeck***, *going through his things.*

Woyzeck: The vest, Andres, it's not part of the uniform. You could do with it. The crucifix is my sister's, the ring too. I've got a holy picture, two hearts and in fine gold. It was in my mother's Bible – with these words:

Let suffering serve as my reward
Through suffering let me serve my God
Your body, Lord, was red and sore
So let my heart be ever more.

My mother feels nothing any more, except when the sun shines on her hand. That's no use.

Andres: (*Rigid, saying 'yeah' to everything*)

Woyzeck: (*Pulls out a piece of paper*) Frederick John Franz Woyzeck, sworn in as infantry man of the second regiment, second battalion, fourth company, born on the Feast of the Annunciation. Today, the twentieth of July, my age is thirty years, seven months and twelve days.

Andres: Franz, you need to go to hospital. You need brandy and a pill – that'll kill the fever.

Woyzeck: Yes, Andres, when the coffin-maker's finished his job, no one knows who'll be in it.

Scene 18

Marie *with girls at the front door.*

Girls: For Candlemas the sun is shining
The corn is high in bloom
They went along the winding street
While walking two and two.
The pipers led the way
The fiddlers at the rear
Red stockings they were wearing.

First child: That's not nice.

Second child: What do you want?

Another: Why were you the first to start?

Another: I can't.

Another: Why?

Another: Because!

Another: 'Cos why?

Another: She has to sing.

Another: Marie, you sing for us.

Marie: Come on little shrimps.
Ring a ring a rosy. King Herod. – Grandmother, tell us a story.

Grandmother: There was once a poor child that had no father and no mother, everything was dead and there was no one left in the world. Everything dead, and it went off and wept day and night. And because there was no one left on earth, the child wanted to go into the sky. The moon looked on it kindly, and when it finally came to the moon it was a piece of rotten wood and then it went to the sun and when it came to the sun it was a faded sunflower and when it came to the stars they were little golden insects fixed on thorns and when it wanted to come back to earth, the earth was an overturned pot and it was all alone and there it sat down and wept and it is still sittting there and is all alone.

Enter ***Woyzeck.***

Woyzeck: Marie!

Marie: (*Startled*) What is it?

Woyzeck: Marie, we have to go, it's time.

Marie: Where to?

Woyzeck: How do I know?

Scene 19

Marie** and **Woyzeck.

Marie: So, that's the town over there. It's dark.

Woyzeck: You have to stay on. Here, sit down.

Marie: But I have to go.

Woyzeck: You don't want to get sore feet.

Marie: You're in a strange mood!

Woyzeck: Do you know how long it is now, Marie?

Marie: Two years at Pentecost.

Woyzeck: Do you know how much time is left?

Marie: I have to go. The dew is starting to fall.

Woyzeck: You feel cold, Marie, and yet you are warm. What hot lips you have. Hot, hot whore's breath, yet I'd give anything to kiss them again. When you are cold you don't *feel* cold any more. You won't feel the cold morning dew.

Marie: What are you saying?

Woyzeck: Nothing. (*Silence*)

Marie: Look how red the moon is.

Woyzeck: Bloody, like a piece of iron.

Marie: What are you going to do? Franz, you are so pale. Franz, stop. For God's sake! Help, help!

Woyzeck: Take that and that! Can't you die? There! There! She's still moving. Not yet? Not yet? Still moving. (*He stabs her again*) Are you dead? Dead! Dead! (*People are coming. He runs away*)

Scene 20

People come.

First Person: Stop!

Second Person: Do you hear? Ssh! Over there.

First Person: Ooh, there! What sort of sound is that?

Second Person: It's the water, it's calling. There's been no drowning for a long time. Let's go. It's not good to hear it.

First Person: Ooh, there it is again. Like someone dying.

Second Person: It's creepy – the scented air – half fog, all grey and the beetles humming like broken bells. Let's go.

First Person: No, it's too clear, too loud. Up there. Come with me.

Scene 21 The Inn

Woyzeck: Dance, all of you, keep it going, sweat and stink. He'll get you all in the end.

(*Sings*)

My landlady's good little maid
Sits in the garden day and night
She sits there in her garden.
Until the clock strikes twelve
And watches out for soldiers.

(*He dances*) So, Kathy, sit down. I'm hot! (*He takes off his jacket*) That's the way it is, the devil takes one and lets the other go. Kathy, you're hot! Why, Kathy, you'll become cold again. Be reasonable. Can't you sing?

Kathy: (*Sings*)

The Swabians' land is not for me
And never would I wear long clothes
To wear long clothes, a pointed shoe
Is not for serving maids to do.

Woyzeck: No, no shoes. Even without shoes you can go to hell.

Kathy: (*Sings*)

You want to pay to get me to bed?
Well, keep your money and go drop dead!

Woyzeck: You're right, I don't want blood on me.

Kathy: But what *is* that on your hand?

Woyzeck: You mean me? Me?

Kathy: Red, blood. (*People gather round*)

Woyzeck: Blood? Blood?

Innkeeper: Uh, blood.

Woyzeck: I think I've cut myself – there on my right hand.

Innkeeper: Then how did it get on your elbow?

Woyzeck: I wiped my hand.

Innkeeper: Wiping your right hand on your right elbow! That's a good trick.

The Idiot: And then the giant said: I smell, I smell some human flesh. Pooh! What a stink!

Woyzeck: Hell, what do you want? What's it to you? Out of my way! The first one to – hell! Do you think I've killed someone? Am I a murderer? What are you looking at? Have a look at yourselves. Out of my way. (*He runs out*)

Scene 22

Children.

First Child: Let's go, Maggie!

Second Child: What's up?

First Child: You don't know? They've all gone out. There's the body of a dead woman out there.

Second Child: Where?

First Child: Left past the boundary line in the forest near the red crucifix.

Second Child: Let's go while there is still time to see it. Otherwise it'll be carried in.

Scene 23

***Woyzeck** alone.*

Woyzeck: The knife? Where's the knife? I left it there. It'll give me away. Closer, still closer. What sort of place is that? What do I hear? There's something moving. Sshh! Just over there. Marie? Hey, Marie! Sshh! Quiet, quiet as death. Why are you so pale, Marie? Why do you have a red cord around your neck? Who gave you the necklace in payment for your sins? You were black with sin, black! Now I have made you pale. Why is your black hair hanging so wildly? Didn't do your plaits today? There's something lying in the grass, cold, wet, silent. Away from here! The knife, the knife, do I have it? Yes! OK! People – over there. (*He runs away*)

Scene 24

Woyzeck *by a pond.*

Woyzeck: So, down in there. (*He throws the knife in*) Down into the dark water like a stone. The moon is like a bloody piece of iron. So, is the whole world going to blab about it? No, it's too close to the shore – when they're bathing … (*He goes into the pond and throws the knife a long way further in*) That's it. But in the summer, when they're diving for mussels – what the hell, it'll get rusty. Who can know what it is. I should have broken it. Is there still blood on me? I'll have to wash myself. There's a spot, and there's another one.

Scene 25

Policeman, Barber, Doctor, Judge.

Policeman: A good murder, a genuine murder, a fine murder, as fine as you could possibly want. It's a long time since we had one like this.[30]

[30] According to Dedner the play could also end with H3,2. Cf. below, Appendix 4.

APPENDIX 1: The Author Of *Woyzeck*

Dates

17 Oct. 1813:	born in Goddelau, Germany.
1822 to 1831:	schooling in Darmstadt.
1831 to 1833:	studied zoology and comparative anatomy at the University of Strasbourg.
1833 to 1834:	continued his studies at the University of Giessen.
March 1835:	fled to Strasbourg to avoid arrest for his political activities and for publishing the illegal pamphlet, *The Hessian Courier.*
Sept-Oct.: 1835	became Doctor of Philosophy at Zurich University and was appointed lecturer in Comparative Anatomy.
19 Feb. 1837:	died of typhus in Zurich at the age of twenty-three.

Büchner: the Man and the Writer

In 1835 Büchner wrote *The Hessian Courier*, in which he urged the peasants to revolt against the oppressive conditions in which they lived. He began work on his novella, *Lenz*, and translated two plays by Victor Hugo. In the same year, in the space of five weeks he wrote the tragedy, *Danton's Death*. In 1836 he wrote the romantic comedy, *Leonce and Lena*. He began work on *Woyzeck* before moving to Zurich, where he died with the play nearing completion.

He was only eighteen when, studying in Strasbourg, he developed an interest in radical politics. He showed a desire to attack the autocratic governments of German states and considered that true reform could not be achieved without violence. Though hounded for his views and forced to live in exile, he was realistic enough to know that the oppressed in Germany were themselves not yet ready to stage any form of revolution. His social concern is strongly voiced in his treatment of the tragic figure, Woyzeck. Both Woyzeck and the woman he murders, Marie, are seen as victims of an oppressive social system.

APPENDIX 2: Who was Woyzeck?

The historical figure is drawn from the social milieu that Büchner found so oppressive. Büchner's Woyzeck character seems to be a composite of three virtually contemporary figures: Daniel Schmolling, who, on 25 September 1817, at the age of thirty-eight, murdered his mistress Henriette Lehne in Berlin; Johann Christian Woyzeck, who, on 21 June 1821, at the age of forty-one, murdered his mistress Johanne Christiane Woost, in Leipzig; and Johann Diess, who, in 1830, at the age of thirty-seven, murdered his mistress, Elisabetha Reuter, near Darmstadt. Guthrie writes: 'All these murderers have certain things in common. They are outsiders. They come from the lower depths of society. They are the subject of scientific and legal debate.'[31]

---

[31] Guthrie, p.6ff.

APPENDIX 3: Dialect or not?

Newer research[32] has thrown light on the function of dialect in *Woyzeck*. Whereas the earliest editors, Karl Emil Franzos (1880) and Bergemann (1926) treated Büchner's language as relatively free of dialect, the Munich edition of 1988 and Poschmann's 1991 edition introduce stronger elements of dialect, so that the trend in recent performances, on stage and film, is to give the use of dialect an exaggerated role.

The most recent research has shown reasons for reverting to earlier practice in this respect. According to Eske Bockelmann and, after him, Thomas Michael Mayer and Burkhard Dedner, the way in which dialect is to be used should be dictated by the nature of the handwriting found in Büchner's manuscripts. When, for example, he writes 'ei' instead of 'ein', this is not necessarily a reflection of Hessian dialect; instead, it is a short-hand which he uses not only for *Woyzeck* but also for his dissertation on Descartes - an academic text which he

[32] Cf. Dedner, p.195ff.

hardly intended to write in dialect.

A similar instance of 'shorthand' which has led to a wrong emphasis on dialect is the (easily misleading) method Büchner employs for handling the succession of perpendicular strokes in writing the 'e' and the 'n' in a word like 'Geschehene' or 'Geschehne'. In the first of these words, there would be six down strokes for the final '-ene', in the second there would be four (two for 'e' and two for 'n'). The shorter (second) version would be common in Hessian dialect, the first would be more usual in formal German. A word like 'benennen' would require fourteen perpendicular strokes – an example which clearly shows how the author, writing hastily, would, instead of writing all fourteen strokes, resort to one long abbreviating stroke ['Verschleifung']. By contrast, on the occasions, such as the row between the neighbours Marie and Margaret, where dialect is appropriate and desirable, Büchner in fact writes the words very clearly, so that there can be no mistaking his intentions.

The conclusion, for translator and director alike, must be to treat Büchner's language as 'normal' German and to introduce dialect in relatively few places. 'Local' colour should not dominate, whether in German or in translation. Finding the right social register – mainly through vocabulary and sentence structure – appears to be more in accordance with Büchner's practice.

APPENDIX 4: A possible addition to Scene 25

***The Idiot*. *Child*. *Woyzeck*.**

Idiot: (*Holds the child in front of him on his lap*) He fell into the water, he fell into the water, no, he fell into the water.
Woyzeck: My boy, Christian.
Idiot: (*Stares at him*) He fell into the water.
Woyzeck: (*Tries to caress the child. It turns away and screams*) Good God!
Idiot: He fell into the water.
Woyzeck: I'll buy you a gingerbread, there's a good boy. (*The child backs away*) (*To the **Idiot***) There, you buy him a gingerbread. (*The **Idiot** stares at him)* Gee up! Gee up, horsey.
Idiot: (*Delighted*) Gee up, horsey! Gee up, horsey! (*Runs off with the child*) [33]

---

[33] This scene is from H3,2, which Dedner (p.40) suggests might follow Scene 25. For the German text cf. Dedner, p.82.

Carysfort Press was formed in the summer of 1998. It receives annual funding from the Arts Council.

The directors believe that drama is playing an ever-increasing role in today's society and that enjoyment of the theatre, both professional and amateur, currently plays a central part in Irish culture.

The Press aims to produce high quality publications which, though written and/or edited by academics, will be made accessible to a general readership. The organisation would also like to provide a forum for critical thinking in the Arts in Ireland, again keeping the needs and interests of the general public in view.

The company publishes contemporary Irish writing for and about the theatre.

Editorial and publishing inquiries to:
Carysfort Press Ltd.,
58 Woodfield,
Scholarstown Road,
Rathfarnham,
Dublin 16,
Republic of Ireland.

T (353 1) 493 7383
E: info@carysfortpress.com
www.carysfortpress.com

HOW TO ORDER

TRADE ORDERS DIRECTLY TO:
eprint Ltd.
35 Coolmine Industrial Estate,
Blanchardstown, Dublin 15.
T: (353 1) 827 8860
E: books@eprint.ie
www.eprint.ie

INDIVIDUAL ORDERS DIRECTLY TO:
eprint Ltd.
35 Coolmine Industrial Estate,
Blanchardstown, Dublin 15.
T: (353 1) 827 8860
E: books@eprint.ie
www.eprint.ie

FOR SALES IN NORTH AMERICA AND CANADA:
Dufour Editions Inc.,
124 Byers Road,
PO Box 7,
Chester Springs,
PA 19425,
USA

T: 1-610-458-5005
F: 1-610-458-7103

Radical Contemporary Theatre Practices by Women in Ireland

Edited by Miriam Haughton and Mária Kurdi

Radical Contemporary Theatre Practices by Women in Ireland is an important contribution to the fields of Irish theatre and performance studies, and gender and performance in Ireland. The essays and interviews explore the work of women directors, designers, and playwrights on both sides of the Irish Border, who are currently shaping theatre practice on the island. By gathering such an impressive range of material, Mária Kurdi and Miriam Haughton have produced a collection that offers a snapshot of radical practice on the Irish stage in the early 21st century.

ISBN 978-1-909325-75-3 €20 (Paperback)

The Theatre of Marie Jones: Telling Stories from the Ground up

Edited by Eugene McNulty and Tom Maguire

Marie Jones is one of the most prolific and popular writers working in Northern Irish theatre today. Her work has achieved local relevance and international recognition. From her earliest work with Charabanc in the early 1980s to the present day, Jones's work has engaged with Irish (and, more often than not, specifically Northern Irish) experience in ways that reveal the extent to which the personal is political in a distinctive form of popular theatre. This volume of essays engages critically with Jones's oeuvre, her reception in Ireland and beyond, and her position in the canon of contemporary drama.

ISBN 78-1-909325-65-4 €20 (Paperback)

Blue Raincoat Theatre Company

By Rhona Trench

Since its foundation in 1991, Blue Raincoat Theatre Company is Ireland's only full-time venue-based professional theatre ensemble and has become renowned for its movement, visual and aural proficiencies and precision. This book explores those signatures from a number of vantage points, conveying the complex challenges faced by Blue Raincoat as they respond to changing aesthetic and economic circumstances. Particular consideration is given to set, costume, sound and lighting design.

ISBN 78-1-909325-67-8 €20 (Paperback)

Across the Boundaries: Talking about Thomas Kilroy

Edited by: Guy Woodward

Thomas Kilroy's long and distinguished career is celebrated in this volume by new essays, panel discussions and an interview, reconsidering the work of one of Ireland's most intellectually ambitious and technically imaginative playwrights. Contributors are drawn from both the academic and theatrical spheres, and include Nicholas Grene, Wayne Jordan, Patrick Mason, Christopher Murray and Lynne Parker.

ISBN 78-1-909325-51-7 €15.00 (Paperback)

Tradition and Craft in Piano-Paying,
by Tilly Fleischmann

Edited by Ruth Fleischmann and John Buckley
DVD Musical examples: Gabriela Mayer

This is a document of considerable historical importance, offering an authoritative account of Liszt's teaching methods as imparted by two of his former students to whom he was particularly close. It contains much valuable information of a kind that is unavailable elsewhere. It records a direct and authentic oral tradition of continental European pianism going back to the nineteenth century.

ISBN 78-1-909325-524 €30 (Paperback)

Wexfour: John Banville, Eoin Colfer, Billy Roche, Colm Toibin

Edited by Ben Barnes
A dedication of four short plays by Wexford writers to celebrate the 40th Anniversary of Wexford Arts Centre.

ISBN 78-1-909325-548 €10

For the Sake of Sanity: Doing things with humour in Irish performance

Edited by Eric Weitz

Humour claims no ideological affiliation – its workings merit inspection in any and every individual case, in light of the who, what, where and when of a joke, including the manner of performance, the socio-cultural context, the dynamic amongst participants, and who knows how many other factors particular to the instance. There as many insights to be gained from the deployment of humour in performance as people to think about it – so herein lie a healthy handful of responses from a variety of perspectives.

For the Sake of Sanity: *Doing things with humour in Irish performance* assembles a range of essays from practitioners, academics, and journalists, all of whom address the attempt to make an audience laugh in various Irish contexts over the past century. With a general emphasis on theatre, the collection also includes essays on film, television and stand-up comedy for those insights into practice, society and culture revealed uniquely through instances of humour in performance.

ISBN 78-1-909-325-56-2 €20

Stanislavski in Ireland: Focus at Fifty

Edited by Brian McAvera and Steven Dedalus Burch

Stanislavski in Ireland: Focus at Fifty is an insight into Ireland's only arthouse theatre from the people who were there. Through interviews, articles, short memoirs and photographs, the book tracks the theatre from its inception, detailing the period under its founder Deirdre O'Connell and then the period following Joe Devlin's arrival as its new artistic director. Many of Ireland's leading theatre and film artists trained and worked at Focus, including Gabriel Byrne, Joan Bergin, Olwen Fouèrè, Brendan Coyle, Rebecca Schull, Johnny Murphy, Sean Campion, Tom Hickey and Mary Elizabeth and Declan Burke-Kennedy. The book comes complete with a chronological list of productions.

ISBN 78-1-909325-43-2 €20

Breaking Boundaries. An Anthology of Original Plays from the Focus Theatre

Edited by Steven Dedalus Burch

Almost from the beginning, since 1970, new plays became part of the Focus's repertory.
Of the seven plays in this anthology, all exhibit a range in styles from Lewis Carroll's fantastical world (*Alice in Wonderland* by Mary Elizabeth Burke-Kennedy), to a couple on the brink of a philandering weekend disaster (*The Day of the Mayfly* by Declan Burke-Kennedy), to a one-man show about Jonathan Swift (*Talking Through His Hat* by Michael Harding), an examination of two shoplifting thieves and the would-be writer who gets in their way (*Pinching For My Soul* by Elizabeth Moynihan), a battle royal between two sides of a world-famous painter (*Francis and Frances* by Brian McAvera), the reactions of multiple New Yorkers to that moment in September, 2011 (*New York Monologues* by Mike Poblete), to the final days of an iconic movie star (*Hollywood Valhalla* by Aidan Harney).

ISBN 78-1-909325-42-5 €20

The Art Of Billy Roche: Wexford As The World

Edited by Kevin Kerrane

Billy Roche – musician, actor, novelist, dramatist, screenwriter – is one of Ireland's most versatile talents. This anthology, the first comprehensive survey of Roche's work, focuses on his portrayal of one Irish town as a microcosm of human life itself, elemental and timeless. Among the contributors are fellow artists (Colm Tóibín, Conor McPherson, Belinda McKeon), theatre professionals (Benedict Nightingale, Dominic Dromgoole, Ingrid Craigie), and scholars on both sides of the Atlantic.

ISBN 78-1-904505-60-0 €20

The Theatre of Conor McPherson: 'Right beside the Beyond'

Edited by Lilian Chambers and Eamonn Jordan

Multiple productions and the international successes of plays like *The Weir* have led to Conor McPherson being regarded by many as one of the finest writers of his generation. McPherson has also been hugely prolific as a theatre director, as a screenwriter and film director, garnering many awards in these different roles. In this collection of essays, commentators from around the world address the substantial range of McPherson's output to date in theatre and film, a body of work written primarily during and in the aftermath of Ireland's Celtic Tiger period. These critics approach the work in challenging and dynamic ways, considering the crucial issues of morality, the rupturing of the real, storytelling, and the significance of space, violence and gender. Explicit considerations are given to comedy and humour, and to theatrical form, especially that of the monologue and to the ways that the otherworldly, the unconscious and supernatural are accommodated dramaturgically, with frequent emphasis placed on the specific aspects of performance in both theatre and film.

ISBN 78 1 904505 61 7 €20

The Story of Barabbas, The Company

Carmen Szabo

Acclaimed by audiences and critics alike for their highly innovative, adventurous and entertaining theatre, Barabbas The Company have created playful, intelligent and dynamic productions for over 17 years. Breaking the mould of Irish theatrical tradition and moving away from a text dominated theatre, Barabbas The Company's productions have established an instantly recognizable performance style influenced by the theatre of clown, circus, mime, puppetry, object manipulation and commedia dell'arte. This is the story of a unique company within the framework of Irish theatre, discussing the influences that shape their performances and establish their position within the history and development of contemporary Irish theatre. This book addresses the overwhelming necessity to reconsider Irish theatre history and to explore, in a language accessible to a wide range of readers, the issues of physicality and movement based theatre in Ireland.

ISBN 78-1-904505-59-4 €25

Irish Drama: Local and Global Perspectives

Edited by Nicholas Grene and Patrick Lonergan

Since the late 1970s there has been a marked internationalization of Irish drama, with individual plays, playwrights, and theatrical companies establishing newly global reputations. This book reflects upon these developments, drawing together leading scholars and playwrights to consider the consequences that arise when Irish theatre travels abroad.

Contributors: Chris Morash, Martine Pelletier, José Lanters, Richard Cave, James Moran, Werner Huber, Rhona Trench, Christopher Murray, Ursula Rani Sarma, Jesse Weaver, Enda Walsh, Elizabeth Kuti

ISBN 78-1-904505-63-1 €20

What Shakespeare Stole From Rome

Edited by Brian Arkins

What Shakespeare Stole From Rome analyses the multiple ways Shakespeare used material from Roman history and Latin poetry in his plays and poems. From the history of the Roman Republic to the tragedies of Seneca; from the Comedies of Platus to Ovid's poetry; this enlightening book examines the important influence of Rome and Greece on Shakespeare's work.

ISBN 78-1-904505-58-7 €20

Polite Forms

Harry White

Polite Forms is a sequence of poems that meditates on family life, remembering and reimagining scenes from childhood and adolescence through the formal composure of the sonnet, so that the uniformity of this framing device promotes a tension. Throughout the collection there is a constant preoccupation with the difference between actual remembrance and the illumination or meaning which poetry can afford. Some of the poems 'rewind the tapes of childhood' across two or three generations, and all of them are akin to pictures at an exhibition which survey individual impressions of childhood and parenthood in a thematically continuous series of portraits drawn from life. This is his first collection of poetry.

Harry White is Professor of Music at University College Dublin.

ISBN 78-1-904505-55-6 €10

Ibsen and Chekhov on the Irish Stage

Edited by Ros Dixon and Irina Ruppo Malone

Ibsen and Chekhov on the Irish Stage presents articles on the theories of translation and adaptation, new insights on the work of Brian Friel, Frank McGuinness, Thomas Kilroy, and Tom Murphy, historical analyses of theatrical productions during the Irish Revival, interviews with contemporary theatre directors, and a round-table discussion with the playwrights, Michael West and Thomas Kilroy.

Ibsen and Chekhov on the Irish Stage challenges the notion that a country's dramatic tradition develops in cultural isolation. It uncovers connections between past productions of plays by Ibsen and Chekhov and contemporary literary adaptations of their works by Irish playwrights, demonstrating the significance of international influence for the formation of national canon.

ISBN 78-1-904505-57-0 €20

Tom Swift Selected Plays

With an introduction by Peter Crawley.

The inaugural production of Performance Corporation in 2002 matched Voltaire's withering assault against the doctrine of optimism with a playful aesthetic and endlessly inventive stagecraft.

Each play in this collection was originally staged by the Performance Corporation and though Swift has explored different avenues ever since, such playfulness is a constant. The writing is precise, but leaves room for the discoveries of rehearsals, the flesh of the theatre. All plays are blueprints for performance, but several of these scripts – many of which are site-specific and all of them slyly topical – are documents for something unrepeatable.

ISBN 78-1-904505-56-3 €20

Synge and His Influences: Centenary Essays from the Synge Summer School

Edited by Patrick Lonergan

The year 2009 was the centenary of the death of John Millington Synge, one of the world's great dramatists. To mark the occasion, this book gathers essays by leading scholars of Irish drama, aiming to explore the writers and movements that shaped Synge, and to consider his enduring legacies. Essays discuss Synge's work in its Irish, European and world contexts – showing his engagement not just with the Irish literary revival but with European politics and culture too. The book also explores Synge's influence on later writers: Irish dramatists such as Brian Friel, Tom Murphy and Marina Carr, as well as international writers like Mustapha Matura and Erisa Kironde. It also considers Synge's place in Ireland today, revealing how *The Playboy of the Western World* has helped to shape Ireland's responses to globalisation and multiculturalism, in celebrated productions by the Abbey Theatre, Druid Theatre, and Pan Pan Theatre Company.

Contributors include Ann Saddlemyer, Ben Levitas, Mary Burke, Paige Reynolds, Eilís Ní Dhuibhne, Mark Phelan, Shaun Richards, Ondřej Pilný, Richard Pine, Alexandra Poulain, Emilie Pine, Melissa Sihra, Sara Keating, Bisi Adigun, Adrian Frazier and Anthony Roche.

ISBN 78-1-904505-50-1 €20.00

Constellations - The Life and Music of John Buckley

Benjamin Dwyer

Benjamin Dwyer provides a long overdue assessment of one of Ireland's most prolific composers of the last decades. He looks at John Buckley's music in the context of his biography and Irish cultural life. This is no hagiography but a critical assessment of Buckley's work, his roots and aesthetics. While looking closely at several of Buckley's compositions, the book is written in a comprehensible style that makes it easily accessible to anybody interested in Irish musical and cultural history. *Wolfgang Marx*

As well as providing a very readable and comprehensive study of the life and music of John Buckley, Constellations also offers an up-to-date and informative catalogue of compositions, a complete discography, translations of set texts and the full libretto of his chamber opera, making this book an essential guide for both students and professional scholars alike.

ISBN 78-1-904505-52-5 €20.00

'Because We Are Poor': Irish Theatre in the 1990s

Victor Merriman

"Victor Merriman's work on Irish theatre is in the vanguard of a whole new paradigm in Irish theatre scholarship, one that is not content to contemplate monuments of past or present achievement, but for which the theatre is a lens that makes visible the hidden malaises in Irish society. That he has been able to do so by focusing on a period when so much else in Irish culture conspired to hide those problems is only testimony to the considerable power of his critical scrutiny." Chris Morash, NUI Maynooth.

ISBN 78-1-904505-51-8 €20.00

Buffoonery and Easy Sentiment': Popular Irish Plays in the Decade Prior to the Opening of The Abbey Theatre

Christopher Fitz-Simon

In this fascinating reappraisal of the non-literary drama of the late 19th - early 20th century, Christopher Fitz-Simon discloses a unique world of plays, players and producers in metropolitan theatres in Ireland and other countries where Ireland was viewed as a source of extraordinary topics at once contemporary and comfortably remote: revolution, eviction, famine, agrarian agitation, political assassination.

The form was the fashionable one of melodrama, yet Irish melodrama was of a particular kind replete with hidden messages, and the language was far more allusive, colourful and entertaining than that of its English equivalent.

ISBN 78-1-9045505-49-5 €20.00

The Theatre of Tom Mac Intyre: 'Strays from the ether'

Eds. Bernadette Sweeney and Marie Kelly

This long overdue anthology captures the soul of Mac Intyre's dramatic canon – its ethereal qualities, its extraordinary diversity, its emphasis on the poetic and on performance – in an extensive range of visual, journalistic and scholarly contributions from writers, theatre practitioners.

ISBN 78-1-904505-46-4 €25

Irish Appropriation Of Greek Tragedy

Brian Arkins

This book presents an analysis of more than 30 plays written by Irish dramatists and poets that are based on the tragedies of Sophocles, Euripides and Aeschylus. These plays proceed from the time of Yeats and Synge through MacNeice and the Longfords on to many of today's leading writers.

ISBN 78-1-904505-47-1 €20

Alive in Time: The Enduring Drama of Tom Murphy

Ed. Christopher Murray

Almost 50 years after he first hit the headlines as Ireland's most challenging playwright, the 'angry youvγ€μαν of those times Tom Murphy still commands his place at the pinnacle of Irish theatre. Here 17 new essays by prominent critics and academics, with an introduction by Christopher Murray, survey Murphy's dramatic oeuvre in a concerted attempt to define his greatness and enduring appeal, making this book a significant study of a unique genius.

ISBN 78-1-904505-45-7 €25

Performing Violence in Contemporary Ireland

Edited by Lisa Fitzpatrick

This interdisciplinary collection of fifteen new essays by scholars of theatre, Irish studies, music, design and politics explores aspects of the performance of violence in contemporary Ireland. With chapters on the work of playwrights Martin McDonagh, Martin Lynch, Conor McPherson and Gary Mitchell, on Republican commemorations and the 90th anniversary ceremonies for the Battle of the Somme and the Easter Rising, this book aims to contribute to the ongoing international debate on the performance of violence in contemporary societies.

ISBN 78-1-904505-44-0 €20

Deviant Acts: Essays on Queer Performance

Ed. David Cregan

This book contains an exciting collection of essays focusing on a variety of alternative performances happening in contemporary Ireland. While it highlights the particular representations of gay and lesbian identity it also brings to light how diversity has always been a part of Irish culture and is, in fact, shaping what it means to be Irish today.

ISBN 978-1-904505-42-6 €20

Plays and Controversies: Abbey Theatre Diaries 2000-2005

Ben Barnes

In diaries covering the period of his artistic directorship of the Abbey, Ben Barnes offers a frank, honest, and probing account of a much commented upon and controversial period in the history of the national theatre. These diaries also provide fascinating personal insights into the day-to- day pressures, joys, and frustrations of running one of Ireland's most iconic institutions.

ISBN 78-1-904505-38-9 €25

Interactions: Dublin Theatre Festival 1957-2007. Irish Theatrical Diaspora Series: 3

Eds. Nicholas Grene and Patrick Lonergan with Lilian Chambers

For over 50 years the Dublin Theatre Festival has been one of Ireland's most important cultural events, bringing countless new Irish plays to the world stage, while introducing Irish audiences to the most important international theatre companies and artists. Interactions explores and celebrates the achievements of the renowned Festival since 1957 and includes specially commissioned memoirs from past organizers, offering a unique perspective on the controversies and successes that have marked the event's history. An especially valuable feature of the volume, also, is a complete listing of the shows that have appeared at the Festival from 1957 to 2008.

ISBN 78-1-904505-36-5 €20

Synge: A Celebration

Edited by Colm Tóibín

A collection of essays by some of Ireland's most creative writers on the work of John Millington Synge, featuring Sebastian Barry, Marina Carr, Anthony Cronin, Roddy Doyle, Anne Enright, Hugo Hamilton, Joseph O'Connor, Mary O'Malley, Fintan O'Toole, Colm Toibin, Vincent Woods.

ISBN 978-1-904505-14-3 €15